Again, a beautiful love story to tell.

Again, a beautiful love story to tell.

> SMILE, WHO KNOWS YOU'LL FIND YOUR TRUE LOVE TOMORROW.

Beblin Arvis

Beblin's Thoughts

Contents

1	Acknowledgements	1
2	Life	2
3	Little Butterfly	3
4	Thanks for being a mother	4
5	BEST FRIENDS	6
6	Be a blue	8
7	Worth having for <3	10
8	Our hearts are near	12
9	Will you go home?	14
10	Moving Forward	15
11	Naughty love	17
12	Pretending	19
13	I know	21
14	Battlefield	23
15	Hey you!	25
16	A beautiful nightmare	27

17	Conquered Love	29
18	Rain or Rainbow	32
19	Someone said I loved you yesterday.	34
20	Ignored	36
21	Is there a next love?	37
22	Only us	38
23	I was told	40
24	I LOVE YOU!	41
25	Move on and go on.	42
26	My favourite	44
27	This time	46
28	Can't Decide	48
29	A promise...	50

1

Acknowledgements

I want to express my gratitude to God for giving me the courage to finally tell the world how I truly feel from time to time. To my family, especially my beautiful sister for always being there to understand and support me in every decision I make. Thank you to all the people who inspire me to write, especially my close friends. To my best friend, Japhet thank you for being a one chat away if I need you and of course to best Arnel for always making an effort to call me even it's impossible to do so. To someone very dear to my heart, thank you for the late-night drives and star gazing if I needed a break and fresh air. This book is simply my love and life stories (in different moods!) that I would like to share with the entire world. I hope that my little happiness, heartaches, and determination to find my true love will inspire you also to fight and keep loving. Happy reading!

-Bloombeblin

2

Life

The unpredictable life,
Clues are nowhere to find,
Neither a sign
Of what will tomorrow look like.
It is a river of surprises,
Oceans of trials,
Lakes of challenges,
Overcome all and reach its glory.
I was a simple girl,
That thought life itself is simple,
But had to travel far,
Only to realise it is a battle place.
That takes your spirit,
Takes your happiness when you lose,
Gain yourself, gain your life,
Only when you win the battle.

Life
Photo from G

3

Little Butterfly

When I was a child,
I don't have to do anything
I just have to play
I just have to sing
When I was a child,
I don't have to make decisions
I just have to live happily
I just have to live life to the fullest.
When I was a child,
I don't have to think of problems
I just have to dance
I just have to feel the fresh air.
Now, I want to be a little butterfly again,
Nothing to do
Nothing to think
I just want to fly happily.

Little Butterfly
Pinterest

Thanks for being a mother

You were the one who holds me for nine months,

Even though I KICK your tomb,

Even though I turned around on your stomach,

You still there, willing to hold my hands until the DAY that I was born.

Now, I didn't KICK your tomb,

I didn't TURN AROUND on your stomach now,

But then you still there to hold my hands

To make me stand when I was about to fall

Again, a beautiful love story to tell.

And of course, YOU were there to scold me up.

But, you know what MOM?

I always UNDERSTAND whenever you did it,

Coz I KNOW your DAUGHTER IS SO NAUGHTY about all things

So, THANK YOU VERY MUCH, MOM.

For being willing to be an INSTRUMENT,

For being a good MOTHER to us...

Last three words I would like to say,

I LOVE YOU, MOM!

BEST FRIENDS

You could say, life is too short,
But for us, it's not a big deal
Because we're living not in a perfect world,
But, in a world that we made perfect for us.

We've shared a lot of memories,
That even you could not replace,
I'm sure anyone could not,
A lifetime experience, we could be proud of.

In good terms and bad terms,
We're together, facing all those bad times,
And savouring those good times,
To make happy memories that we could share in the future.

Again, a beautiful love story to tell.

Well, we could say our life is not perfect,
But because God gave us each other,
We're proudly saying that if ever I'll choose a partner,
The best partners in my life, are my best friends.

\
6

Be a blue

Be a blue that is trustable,
A friend that is willing to be a shoulder.
An enemy that has one word,
A man that listens to his fellowmen.

Be a blue that seeks peace and tranquillity,
A compatriot that hates war.
A lady that longs for rest
A bird that looks for freedom.

Be a blue that bridge understanding,

A teacher that makes an instrument for a child.

That needs to grasp something about the world.

Someone that desires freedom to express his love.

Be a blue that loves things from the past,

A blue that always gives value to his yesterday.

A blue that always moves back to his history

Be a colour that lights life.

7

Worth having for <3

Life worth of living for,
Life worth of laughter for,
Life worth of treasure for
Is worth having.

Journey worth of walking for,
Journey worth of remembering for,
Journey worth of continuing for
Is worth having.

Things worth of making an effort for,
Things worth of spending time for,
Things worth of sacrifices for
Is worth having.

Again, a beautiful love story to tell.

Someone worth of loving for,
Someone worth of caring for,
Someone worth of appreciating for
Is worth having.

8

Our hearts are near

Love was found,
To the person who truly deserves it.
Love was felt,
To a different person.

"I don't know what love is,
Until I met you",
Words that keep running in my tired head,
Trying to remember how you've said it.

For some reason, a stranger like you,
Have become my favourite person,
Only a dear friend,

That becomes my everything.

"I love you; you are my life",

Strong words that made my heart contented,

That even if you're far,

You are near; our hearts are near.

Will you go home?

Each day that passed by,
I miss you,
I look at someone,
I see you.

Each minute of my life
I think about you,
This isn't me,
I'm getting crazy over you.

Every second I breathe,
I'm struggling to live,
I don't know how to handle this,
But don't worry I'm fighting.

Every time I'm not with you,
It feels so strange,
It is totally different,
Come back and be my home.

Home
Photo from G

10

Moving Forward

Now, my life is nothing,
My soul is gone,
My happiness has left me,
How can I continue life without you?

Give me reasons to continue living,
Give me reasons why I need to stand still,
Give me reasons to forget bad memories,
Give me reasons to move forward.

Why life so bad at me?

Why life need to challenge me this hard?
Why life tries to pull me down always?
Is life the same with others?

Now, tell me, do I still need to live?
Now, tell me, is there anything left of life?
Now, tell me, how can I move forward?
When the whole world is telling me to move back.

Naughty love

One song tells me to love,
Another tells me to stop loving,
One song tells me to cherish memories,
Another tells me to forget.

Mr. cupid is laughing at me,
I was fooled by love,
I was deceived by fake love,
This arrow goes straight to my heart.

This love that drives me crazy,
This love that changes me,
This love that inspires me,
This love makes me happy.

This thing that makes my life meaningful,
This thing that gives me a reason to live,
This thing that makes me occupied,
This thing called naughty love.

12

Pretending

*In a world full of complications
Everyone has to lie,
Everybody has to pretend,
Pretend that their life doesn't have complexity.*

*In a world full of lies,
Everyone has to find the truth,
Everybody needs to seek truthfulness from within,
Nothing else, but the truth.*

*In a world full of war,
Everyone has to fight,
Everybody needs to be strong to win,*

Win to survive.

In a world full of pretentious,
Everyone has to play the game of life.
Everybody needs to act well.
Act well to hide all the pains.

13

I know

I know the fact that I can't have you.
I know the fact that we can't be together.
I know the fact that you will choose her.
I know the fact that there is no us.

I know the fact that you are just a dream.
I know the fact that I need to pick up myself someday.
I know the fact that this won't last.

I know the fact that you'll be gone in my life.
I know the fact that it is all temporary.
I know the fact that I am stupid.
I know the fact that you wouldn't choose me.

I know the fact that I'll get hurt.

I know the fact that it isn't right.

But I didn't know the fact that it will be this painful.

When you say "we don't have tomorrow".

14

Battlefield

Who doesn't want to experience love?

Probably those who got hurt by it.

Probably, the ones who fell in love with the wrong person.

The ones who got broken and hope was taken.

People who got inspired by,

People whose lives were changed,

People who want to be a better one,

Are people who don't want love to end.

But life is tough,

Love is powerful,

It can make you a different person.

It does not matter what way, but it will.

Sometimes I get to think,

How people endure the pain of love,

Even though how many times they fall and defeated,

They still choose to be on the battlefield.

15

Hey you!

Hey you!
Yes, you!
You that makes me happy,
You that gives light to my life.

Hey you!
Thank you!
Thank you for being there always,
Thank you for the love you gave me.

Hey you!
Yes, you!
You that stopped loving me.
You that broke the promise.

Hey you!
Thank you!
Thank you for the lesson learned,
Thank you for making me stronger than ever.

16

A beautiful nightmare

The night is quiet,
The skies are light,
The stars are bright,
What a moonlit night.

I decided to walk,
To feels its beauty
To spoil me,
To think deeply.

Suddenly, you came along,
Through my imagination,
Holding my hands,
Memory starts flashing.

Reach the end of tonight,
Means waking up from reality,
Those were only memories,
Memories I cannot forget.

(Thank you Buddy Lepora for the beautiful title)

17

Conquered Love

I wanted this poem to be perfect,
It seems like I don't even have a word to say
Every time I think of you I get pissed.
Yes, sometimes I wonder if this is love.

Our love story isn't a fairytale,
We have more fights than peace,
The language we used is different.
It is more on war starting after one another.

One great thing in this love story,
No one gives up, until now.
Our breakups are uncountable.
For that, I truly admire your patience.

As you know, I have bad habits.
Throwing bad languages to push you away,
Most of the time, I crossed the line.
You know, for me, its the only way to get out.

I am hurting your feelings to suit myself.
It feels good, not for long, though.
See, because by the end of the day.
My heart still belongs to you.

Baby, I can be stubborn all the time,
I can say a lot of cursed,
But, trust me when I say,
I hate myself for being me.

The lady that wants to show the world,
She is strong and can conquer the world,
You know, deep inside, I am the weakest.
Weakest among them all.

When I get hurt, I tried to give the pain back.
But there you are, taking it all,
I'm sorry if I'm too much.
I can't promise, I can take it easy on you.

Again, a beautiful love story to tell.

One thing for sure, I will love you, eternally.
Seriously, I don't want to lose you.
You see me as a different person,
You love me the way that shows the real me.

I know this poem is a bit of a messed up.
Surely, this is the way I wanted it.
Telling the world, there's no perfect couple.
But there's US, conquering love.

18

Rain or Rainbow

The world is in chaos,
The sun doesn't seem to rise,
The heaven is covered,
It is covered with darkness.

So my life is in chaos too,
In doubt how to calm it,
I can hear thunders,
A storm is about to pour.

Raindrop slowly,
The wind is blowing strong,
Yet, what is this,
I don't feel the rain dropping.

I looked up and saw you,
You showed up,
Patiently protecting me,

Again, a beautiful love story to tell.

Trying to rescue my weariness.

Trying to cover me,
Then, the rain stopped suddenly,
I saw the ray of sun showing.
Rainbow made an appearance.

19

Someone said I loved you yesterday.

When you said those magic words,
It didn't only gave me butterflies,
It gives me hope,
Completely healed my broken heart.

My heart runs so fast,
And so yours too,
That's when I realised
It was true.

I found myself,
I found myself, yet again,
Falling in love,
To the right person.

Again, a beautiful love story to tell.

I hoped that heaven,
Hear my prayer,
Give us the blessings,
To love each other.

20

Ignored

I'm crying, but he refuses to listen
I'm hurt, but he refuses to care
He knew I'm having pain,
He knew I'm breaking,
Yet, he wasn't bothered,
I hold my tears for long,
I knew he felt it,
Yet, he let me suffer
I told him I need him,
He chose to walk away.
Now, my heart is shuttered.
I knew he wouldn't fix it.
Is he still worth it?
Is letting go the best option?
Best option to live.

21

Is there a next love?

It's been a while since I felt love,
Butterflies used to dance on my stomach,
My eyes used to shine when it sees you,
I used to be the happiest person in the world,

For a while, I know how to love and be loved.
However, those times brought me pains too,
A pain that will forever be remembered,
It was a good pain.

Things that I don't understand in the world,
Is now explained and have clarity,
I'll stand up and use its teachings to win,
Win all the battles of my next love.

22

Only us

Love, I tried to forget you.
I tried not to think of you every time,
I tried so hard not to say your name,
I tried everything to get rid of you.

It seems like you are the strongest stone,
So hard to break even if I talk to the ocean,
I even tried to delete all captured photographs,
I guess memories will remain for a lifetime.

I keep hearing this cliche in my mind,
'True love is hard to forget', actually, no.
It cannot be forgotten, it will stay.
It will stay forever until we die.

I keep telling myself there is no fairytale,
But it's funny I felt like a princess,
With a gentle prince loving me the same way,

Again, a beautiful love story to tell.

It seems like its too good to be true.

I used to get hurt because of reality,
I guess, my heart is stronger than ever,
It doesn't mean I'm ignoring the truth,
I just learnt how to understand you better.

So my love, go on with your life,
After all, our unconditional love is special.
It meant something extraordinary,
ONLY we can understand.

I was told

I was told by many to give up,
I was told to surrender my love,
I was told to quit and find new love,
I was confused, but I didn't.

I was told you are not my happiness,
I was told I could find better,
I was told to wake up and stop holding,
I was scared, but I didn't.

I was told of many negatives,
I was told to let you go,
I was told to finished "us",
I am not sure of everything, but I won't.

24

I LOVE YOU!

Every second I think of you.
I whisper to winds to pass you the message.
A message that hopefully will make you smile.
I told birds to sing "I LOVE YOU" to you each morning.

We fight every other day.
But its okay, our love is stronger.
Each day is getting better,
I told the butterflies how much I LOVE YOU.

We may be in the distance,
Just hold on, time will come.
Love will permit us to be together.
The time when I can say to you I LOVE YOU in person.

25

Move on and go on.

Each day in my life,

From the time we've been apart,

I was lost,

I never went back yet,

I don't know the way.

Maybe I asked too much,

Maybe I expect too much,

But you know what I realised?

There are 52 weeks in a year,

That means there are 365 days,

8760 hours,

Again, a beautiful love story to tell.

525,600 minutes,

31,536,000 seconds in a year.

I never did ask you,

To make me your priority,

I don't have the right to do so,

But a single text,

To make my day complete.

Maybe I have to give up now,

Maybe I have to let go now,

Maybe I have to stop,

Move on and go on.

26

My favourite

Every love story is unique,
Like music,
Has its own definition,
Its own story to tell.

The sound of every line,
The rhythm of its melody,
The meaning of the lyrics,
Depends on who's listening.

I'll whisper you my story,
Through this poem and its line
A story that is not perfect,
And maybe a tragic.

The thrill of trying to fight,
Trying to right what is wrong.
And, the unconditional love,

Again, a beautiful love story to tell.

Is what makes it perfect.

We might not end up together,
We might not get any chance,
Remember, please do so,
Our love story will always be my favourite.

27

This time

Once again, I opened my heart.
Without realising,
Day by day,
I care so much.

My heart is confused,
Confused about what is right or wrong,
Whether to step back,
Whether to keep going.

Faith seems to be punishing me,
I thought I am stronger,
I thought I could choose my path,
I thought I am brave to hold back.

I have picked up myself again,
After healing my soul,
I thought I am bolder to face the world,

Again, a beautiful love story to tell.

I could keep going.

Then one day,
I have you in front of me,
The same mess,
The same situation.

Love, please help me.
Fight for our love,
Fight for our happiness,
Even the world is against it.

Can't Decide

Yes, I have doubts.
I have buts and what-ifs.
Too many questions to asked,
Too many things to think.

Then, every time I hear you laugh,
Every time I hold your hand,
Every time I hug you tight,
My senses are just not right.

My heart can't decide,
I'm trying so hard,
Not to love you more,
To protect my heart.

Again, a beautiful love story to tell.

*My heart was torn to pieces,
Once when I loved too much,
Now, I'm afraid, every day,
Cause I love you more each day.*

*Whether I have to stop or continue,
Cry out loud this early,
Hope to have a different story,
With a different ending to our love story.*

29

A promise...

Each day that has passed,
I get to know you better,
I get to know the true you,
Slowly, my heart is falling for you.

I know it will be hard,
I know it's not going to be easy,
I know it's going to be a long journey,
As long as you're with me.

We'll get through this together,
We'll achieve our dreams,
We'll build our future,
Together, forever.

Again, a beautiful love story to tell.

When you said,
You'll always be there.
I trust you.
I'll trust the promise, forever.

www.ingramcontent.com/pod-product-compliance
Ingram Content Group UK Ltd.
Pitfield, Milton Keynes, MK11 3LW, UK
UKHW021253180426
11947UKWH00010B/751